UNAFRAID
LEADER GUIDE

Unafraid:
Living with Courage and Hope in Uncertain Times

Unafraid
978-1-5247-6033-5 *Hardcover*
978-1-5247-6034-2 *e-Book*

Unafraid: DVD
978-1-5018-5375-3

Unafraid: Leader Guide
978-1-5018-5373-9
978-1-5018-5374-6 *e-Book*

Unafraid: Youth Leader Guide
978-1-5018-5382-1
978-1-5018-5383-8 *e-Book*

Unafraid: Children's Leader Guide
978-1-5018-5384-5

Also from Adam Hamilton

24 Hours That Changed the World

Christianity and World Religions

Christianity's Family Tree

Confronting the Controversies

Creed

Enough

Faithful

Final Words from the Cross

Forgiveness

Half Truths

John

Leading Beyond the Walls

Love to Stay

Making Sense of the Bible

Moses

Not a Silent Night

Revival

Seeing Gray in a World of Black and White

Selling Swimsuits in the Arctic

Speaking Well

The Call

The Journey

The Way

Unleashing the Word

When Christians Get It Wrong

Why?

For more information, visit www.AdamHamilton.org.

UNAFRAID

LIVING WITH

COURAGE AND HOPE IN

UNCERTAIN TIMES

ADAM HAMILTON

Leader Guide
by Alex Joyner

Abingdon Press / Nashville

Unafraid
Living with Courage and Hope in Uncertain Times
Leader Guide

This book is printed on elemental chlorine-free paper.

ISBN 978-1-5018-5373-9

18 19 20 21 22 23 24 25 26 27 — 10 9 8 7 6 5 4 3 2 1
MANUFACTURED IN THE UNITED STATES OF AMERICA

CONTENTS

TO THE LEADER

You have a wonderful opportunity as the leader of this group! In the course of five sessions, you will get to know and lead a group of learners into some of the most important areas of their lives. Using this resource and the others in this study, you will also help the participants discover the resources in their lives and their faith to live more boldly and freely without fear.

This study is based on Adam Hamilton's book, *Unafraid: Living with Courage and Hope in Uncertain Times*. Adam Hamilton is the senior pastor of the Church of the Resurrection in Leawood, Kansas, one of the largest and fastest-growing United Methodist congregations in the United States. He has numerous books and publications to his name and has a reputation for tackling difficult issues with clarity, theological insight, biblical grounding, and a pastor's touch.

In this study, Adam focuses on an issue that is pervasive in our contemporary culture: fear. From existential questions of death and illness to social anxieties to major political and social upheavals, this experienced pastor addresses the anxieties and worries that so many of us face every day and helps us understand how to acknowledge fear without letting our lives be controlled by it.

One key feature of Hamilton's book is a simple acronym—FEAR—which can be used to consider the many fears we confront. Your group will return to this acronym throughout the study, and as participants become familiar with it, they will draw confidence from their faith and grow in their trust of God.

As leader of this group, you will find the following lesson plans easy to use with material sufficient for every session. In fact, you may have more than you need, so you can choose from the options in the "Learning Together" sections in order to adapt the study to your group and your allotted time.

The study includes five sessions, and it makes use of the following components:

- the book *Unafraid: Living with Courage and Hope in Uncertain Times;*
- the DVD that accompanies the study; and
- this leader guide.

The five sessions in this study correspond to the five parts of the *Unafraid* book. Each of the five book parts consists of four chapters, and so each week, participants will be asked to read four book chapters in preparation for the session.

If possible, notify those interested in the study in advance of the first session. Make arrangements for them to get copies of the book, so they can read Part One of the book (Chapters 1–4) before the first group meeting.

Using This Guide with Your Group

Because no two groups are alike, this guide has been designed to give you flexibility and choice in tailoring the sessions for your group. The session format is listed below. You may choose any or all of the activities, using them as you wish to meet the schedule and needs of your particular group.

The leader guide offers a basic session plan designed to be completed in a session of about 45 minutes. Select ahead of time which activities the group will do, for how long, and in what order. Depending on the activities you select, there may be special preparation needed. The leader is alerted in the session plan when advance preparation is needed.

Session Format

Planning the Session

Session Goals
Scriptural Foundation
Special Preparation

Getting Started

Opening Activity
Opening Prayer

Learning Together

Video Study and Discussion
Book and Bible Study and Discussion

Wrapping Up

Closing Activity
Closing Prayer

Helpful Hints

Preparing for the Session

- Pray for the leading of the Holy Spirit as you prepare for the study. Pray for discernment for yourself and for each member of the study group.
- Before each session, familiarize yourself with the content. Read the book chapters again.
- Depending on the length of time you have available for group meetings, you may or may not have time to do all the activities. Select the activities in advance that will work for your group time and interests.

- Choose the session elements you will use during the group session, including the specific discussion questions you plan to cover. Be prepared, however, to adjust the session as group members interact and as questions arise. Prepare carefully, but allow space for the Holy Spirit to move in and through the group members and through you as facilitator.
- Prepare the room where the group will meet so that the space will enhance the learning process. Ideally, group members should be seated around a table or in a circle so that all can see each other. Moveable chairs are best because the group will sometimes be forming pairs or small groups for discussion. Special seating arrangements for some sessions are also suggested in the planning notes.
- Bring a supply of Bibles for those who forget to bring their own.
- For most sessions, you will also need a chalkboard and chalk, a whiteboard and markers, or an easel with large sheets of paper and markers.

Shaping the Learning Environment

- Begin and end on time.
- Create a climate of openness, encouraging group members to participate as they feel comfortable.
- Remember that some people will jump right in with answers and comments, while others need time to process what is being discussed.
- If you notice that some group members seem never to be able to enter the conversation, ask them if they have thoughts to share. Give everyone a chance to talk, but keep the conversation moving. Moderate to prevent a few individuals from doing all the talking.
- Communicate the importance of group discussions and group exercises.
- If no one answers at first during discussions, do not be afraid of silence. Count silently to ten, then say something such as, "Would anyone like to go first?" If no one responds, venture an answer yourself and ask for comments.

- Model openness as you share with the group. Group members will follow your example. If you limit your sharing to a surface level, others will follow suit.
- Encourage multiple answers or responses before moving on.
- To help continue a discussion and give it greater depth, ask, "Why?" or "Why do you believe that?" or "Can you say more about that?"
- Affirm others' responses with comments such as "Great" or "Thanks" or "Good insight," especially if it's the first time someone has spoken during the group session.
- Monitor your own contributions. If you are doing most of the talking, back off so that you do not train the group to listen rather than speak up.
- Remember that you do not have all the answers. Your job is to keep the discussion going and encourage participation.

Managing the Session

- Honor the time schedule. If a session is running longer than expected, get consensus from the group before continuing beyond the agreed-upon ending time.
- Involve group members in various aspects of the group session, such as saying prayers or reading the Scripture.
- Note that the session guides sometimes call for breaking into smaller groups or pairs. This gives everyone a chance to speak and participate fully. Mix up the groups; don't let the same people pair up for every activity.
- As always in discussions that may involve personal sharing, confidentiality is essential. Group members should never pass along stories that have been shared in the group. Remind the group members at each session: Confidentiality is crucial to the success of this study.

1

UNDERSTANDING AND COUNTERING FEAR

Planning the Session

Session Goals

As a result of conversations and activities connected with this session, group members should begin to

- examine the role fear plays in the lives of contemporary people;
- explore biblical perspectives on fear and how God's people have been liberated from its power;
- experience faith as the critical background for understanding and controlling fear; and
- understand the goals for the study more clearly.

Scriptural Foundation

> Do not fear, for I am with you,
> do not be afraid, for I am your God;
> I will strengthen you, I will help you,
> I will uphold you with my victorious right hand.
>
> (Isaiah 41:10 NRSV)

Special Preparation

- Prepare the room with the seating arranged in a circle so everyone will be able to see each other.
- Create a small worship space in the center of the circle with visual reminders of God's presence. This could include a cross, a candle, or a Bible.
- Have name tags available as well as pens and markers.
- Have available index cards, paper, and pens or pencils.
- On a large sheet of paper that can be posted in the room, print the following question for the opening activity:
  o Where do you hold your fear?
- On another large sheet of paper (or several), print the following statements:
  o "False fears and unhealthy worry ... keep us from living well."
  o "So many of us live our entire lives paralyzed by fear, just a mile from the Promised Land."
- On another sheet of paper, print the verse above (Isaiah 41:10), broken into four lines as shown.
- Have another blank sheet of paper posted on the wall for the acronym activity. (Once completed, you can retain this paper for use in future weeks.)

Getting Started

Opening Activity

As participants arrive, greet them and invite them into the circle of chairs. Especially if it is a newly formed group, have each person write his or her name on a name tag and put it on. Begin the session with brief introductions.

Invite group members to consider the question posted on the wall: Where do you hold your fear? Note for the group that fear and stress have physical manifestations that we can feel when we are aware. Ask volunteers to share how they would answer the question.

As preparation for prayer, invite participants to get into a sitting pose that they can maintain comfortably for several minutes. Use the following suggestions to guide participants through a visualization:

- Place both feet on the floor and sit upright with your hands resting loosely on your thighs.
- Close your eyes and sense where there is tension in your body. It may be in your shoulders, neck, chest, or elsewhere.
- Visualize that tension as a brightly colored web of energy.
- Try to relax the part of your body that is holding the tension. As you do, imagine the colored energy moving to the palms of your hands.
- Make a fist with your hands and hold the energy tightly for a few seconds.
- Now open your hands, palms upward, and release that energy to God as we pray.

Opening Prayer

Pray together, using the following prayer, or one of your own choosing:

God who calms the troubled waters, we bless you for your presence in the midst of our fears and trials. We release to you the things we hold too tightly, and we trust your words of peace. Be among us in this session, and may our souls and bodies be secure in you. Amen.

Learning Together

Video Study and Discussion

In video Session 1, Adam Hamilton introduces us to Carlos, Ginger, and Marie, three people who face fears just as we all do. Afterward, he talks with a neuroscientist, Dr. David Zald of Vanderbilt University and asks how our brains play a role in how we experience fear. Dr. Zald is Cornelius Vanderbilt Professor of Psychology and Psychiatry and the Director of the Interdisciplinary Neuoscience Program for Undergraduates. Discuss:

- What are the fears expressed by the three people in the beginning of the video? How have these fears been a part of your own life?
- How does the faith of the people interviewed help them confront fear?
- Why does Dr. Zald say that fear "clearly is a gift"?
- What are some of the ways that Dr. Zald suggests for treating anxiety and worry?

Book and Bible Study and Discussion

Examine the Role of Fear in Our Lives

Ask a volunteer to read aloud the first two paragraphs of Chapter 1 in the book. Point out that Adam Hamilton lifts up the prevalence of worry, anxiety, and fear in our lives. Later in Chapter 1, he notes that many of the people who responded to his church's survey reported moderate or significant levels of fear. Discuss:

- What are the aspects of contemporary life that make people fearful?
- In Chapter 2, Hamilton says that fear may play a role in keeping us safe. Talk about a time when fear kept you safe.
- Hamilton also identifies false fears and unhealthy worry as things that can keep us from living well. When have you experienced your fear as something that kept you from living well?
- In talking about the promise of this book in Chapter 1, Hamilton expresses confidence that we can learn to address our fears, control them, and learn from them. What tools do you already have that help you deal with your fear? What are your hopes for this study?

Study a Biblical Perspective on Fear

Read aloud Numbers 13:32-33, and encourage the group to glance back over the first few paragraphs of the chapter. Discuss:

- What were the fears that kept the people from entering the Promised Land?
- Why do you think the people listened to the ten pessimistic spies rather than to the two spies who assured them that God was with them?
- Hamilton says, a little later in Chapter 3, that our visions of a Promised Land, or of a future we would like to see, can be clouded by our assumptions about the risks and dangers involved so that we can become paralyzed by the obstacles. When have you seen a group become paralyzed by risks and dangers? When have *you* been paralyzed by risks and dangers?

Now have the group visualize the situation of the Israelites as they sat one mile from the Promised Land.

- What hopes and dreams had the Israelites had for the land?
- What would their lives be like as nomadic people living in the wilderness?

As a group, choose a contemporary situation that causes a great deal of fear. Discuss together what "preferred future" lies beyond our fears.

- What would it mean to "stare down the giants" of our fears in this situation?
- What would our lives be like if we do not stare them down?

Define Faith

Have someone read Hebrews 11:1: "Faith is the reality of what we hope for, the proof of what we don't see." Discuss:

- What does this definition of faith tell us about the nature of faith?

In Chapter 3, Adam Hamilton talks about one aspect of faith as trust or confidence that things will get better despite whatever circumstances we face in the current moment.

- How does this definition compare with the definition in Hebrews 11:1?
- In what ways is it different?

In relating the story of Jeff, the corporate executive who lost his job, Hamilton describes how Jeff wrote his way to finding faith. Then, by acting on his faith, Jeff overcame his fears.

- What would an action plan look like for overcoming your own fears?

Consider the FEAR Acronym as a Tool for Confronting Fear

At the close of Chapter 3, Adam Hamilton introduces an acronym outlining four steps we will be exploring through the course of this study. Have a volunteer come to the blank sheet of paper on the wall and write out each of the statements that make up the acronym:

> **F**ace your fears with faith.
> **E**xamine your assumptions in light of the facts.
> **A**ttack your anxieties with action.
> **R**elease your cares to God.

As the volunteer finishes writing each line, read it aloud as a group. Acknowledge for the group, as Hamilton does, that an acronym can seem like a flimsy response to the fears that we have, but it is one way to move us to action and out of paralysis. Discuss the acronym together:

- What about the four steps seems unclear right now? What more do you want to know?
- Which of these steps seems most difficult to you? Why?

Give each person an index card and a pen. Invite them to write the acronym on the card and take it with them. Challenge them to put the card in a visible place in their home (perhaps by a mirror they use each morning). Ask them to look at the card daily through the course of this study.

Imagine Your Own ThunderShirt

In the closing section of Chapter 4, Adam Hamilton describes a vest called a ThunderShirt that his family puts on their small dog, Maybelle, when there are thunderstorms in the area. Review this section and have participants discuss experiences when they have had to comfort a distressed pet.

- What actions seem to help?
- Why do you imagine that a ThunderShirt calms Maybelle?

Read again Philippians 4:5b-7 (the passage printed in the section titled "Maybelle's ThunderShirt"):

The Lord is near. Don't be anxious about anything; rather, bring up all of your requests to God in your prayers and petitions, along with giving thanks. Then the peace of God that exceeds all understanding will keep your hearts and minds safe in Christ Jesus.

Discuss the following:

- What promises are contained in these verses?
- What advice does Paul offer to the Philippian Christians?

Hamilton lists a number of spiritual practices that have a calming effect for many people, such as prayer, reading Scripture, singing hymns, and meditation.

- How have you experienced these practices as calming?

Now invite group members to reflect on a physical reminder of God's presence and the call to prayer. Perhaps the reminder is a piece of jewelry, a wristband, or a cross placed in a prominent spot in their home. Maybe it is an actual ThunderShirt—a sweatshirt or sweater they can wear for prayer time. Maybe it is a chair or corner devoted to prayer and Bible reading.

Ask group members to follow up in some way on this visualization by locating or creating this physical reminder. Ask them to use it during the course of the study and to observe how it affects their approach to their fears and their relationship with God.

Invite volunteers to share their ideas and intentions with the group.

Wrapping Up

Before the closing activity, tell participants that next week's session will be based on Part Two (Chapters 5–8) of the *Unafraid* book. Ask them to read as much of Part Two as they can during the coming week.

Closing Activity

Remind group members about the model of "conversational prayer" that Adam Hamilton illustrates in the section of Chapter 4 titled "Praying the Scriptures." Direct attention to Isaiah 41:10, written on the paper on the wall.

Ask participants to take a smaller piece of paper and use it to compose a prayer conversation with God that is inspired by the Isaiah verse. Suggest that they write a line of the verse to be spoken by "God" and then respond to it with a line or two of their own, expressing their response and spoken by "Me." Alternate lines of the verse with lines expressing their responses.

Encourage participants to be honest in their prayers, offering their true selves to God. Some may want to express their mistrust or skepticism in the course of talking with God. Assure them that this exercise is entirely between God and themselves. They will not be asked to share what they write.

Closing Prayer

Offer the following prayer or one of your own:

God of peace, you know our fears before we speak. You know how fragile our faith is and how difficult our struggles are to trust you more. For faith like a mustard seed in a fearful world, we pray. Amen.

2

CRIME, RACISM, TERRORISM, AND POLITICS

Planning the Session

Session Goals

As a result of conversations and activities connected with this session, group members should begin to

- explore contemporary events and trends that engender fear in contemporary people, including questions of crime, race, terrorism, and politics;
- examine the biblical roots of courageous compassion and envision actions to incorporate this quality in their lives and community of faith;

- understand, using insights of cognitive therapy, the way disordered thoughts can contribute to fear; and
- appreciate and utilize the practice of *lectio divina* as a means of grace that addresses the spiritual injury caused by fear.

Scriptural Foundation

God is our refuge and strength,
> a help always near in times of great trouble.
That's why we won't be afraid when the world falls apart. ...

Nations roar; kingdoms crumble.
> God utters his voice; the earth melts.
The LORD of heavenly forces is with us!
> The God of Jacob is our place of safety.

(Psalm 46:1-2a, 6-7)

Special Preparation

- Prepare the room with seating arranged in a large semicircle with an open area for the performance suggested in the opening activities.
- Bring several recent newspapers and spread them out around your meeting area. If you get your news online, print out recent headlines from several newspaper websites.
- Have a large sheet of blank paper posted on the wall or in a visible place in the room. Have markers for writing on it.
- The exercise titled "Test Out Thoughts About Crime" includes the option of exploring crime statistics for your community. The U.S. Department of Justice maintains a site for collecting reported crime information from most communities in the United States at https://www.ucrdatatool.gov/Search/Crime/Crime.cfm. Use this resource to create a small table that you can share as a handout or as a poster for the wall.
- The exercise titled "Get To Know Your Neighbors" suggests using a map of your community. If you have one available, bring it and place it in a visible location in your meeting space.

- Have available a number of Bibles or copies of Psalm 46:1-2a, 6-7 on a handout. Also have available paper and pens or pencils for writing.

Write the lines of the FEAR acronym (printed below) on a large sheet of paper and hang it in a visible location for your group. (If you still have it, you can use the paper from last session's acronym exercise.) Retain the paper for use in future sessions.

Face your fears with faith.
Examine your assumptions in light of the facts.
Attack your anxieties with action.
Release your cares to God.

Getting Started

Opening Activity

As participants arrive, greet them and ask if anyone has had any experience doing improvisational acting. Ask for volunteers to do a brief improv based on the story of Henny Penny, which Adam Hamilton relates at the beginning of Chapter 8. Assign the following roles: Henny Penny, a rooster, a goose, a duck, a turkey, and the fox. (If you do not have enough group members to fill all the roles, you may reduce the number of characters beyond Henny Penny and the fox.)

Ask for a group member to read the scenario as Hamilton relates it in the second and third paragraphs of Chapter 8. Then have the volunteers act it out in their own way. Encourage them to have fun and bring out their inner "ham"!

Following the performance, applaud the actors and thank them. Then discuss the following questions briefly:

- How did fear lead Henny Penny and her friends to a bad end?
- Why did they not see the real danger that threatened them?
- What is an issue today that leads people to act like Henny Penny and her friends?

Share with the group that today's session will focus on things and events around us that can lead us to distorted thinking about the dangers we face. We will also explore how we can trust God.

Opening Prayer

Pray together, using the following prayer or one of your own:

Creator God, who set the stars in the heavens, give us the ears to hear the drumbeat of your steadfast love upholding the universe. Renew our senses so that we can be attuned to your ways. For courage in these days, we pray. Amen.

Learning Together

Video Study and Discussion

In video Session 2, Adam Hamilton explores the question of how we overcome our fear of other people. He discusses strategies for confronting these fears with his guests, Carlos, Ginger, and Marie. Then Adam talks with William H. Willimon about why Willimon wrote his 2016 book *Fear of the Other*. Willimon is Professor of the Practice of Christan Ministry at Duke Divinity School and a bishop in The United Methodist Church. Discuss:

- How did Carlos see the impulse to protect his culture as a help and a hindrance in overcoming fear of others?
- What role did gaining knowledge play for Ginger in overcoming misunderstandings about followers of Islam?
- What is xenophobia, and how does Bishop Willimon see it affecting our national life?
- How is the act of welcoming the other a witness to what Christ has done for us?

Book and Bible Study and Discussion

Explore What Makes Us Fearful in the News

Point out the recent newspapers or printed headlines spread around your meeting area (see "Special Preparation"). Ask volunteers to scan the headlines and read out ones that they feel would cause fear, worry, or anxiety in readers. How great a percentage of the stories on the front page seem to fall into this category? Discuss the following questions as a group:

- Do you feel more anxious or less anxious after reading the news in these headlines? Why?
- What is your most trusted news source? How do its reports shape your thinking and feelings about the world?
- Adam Hamilton says that facts can be allies in combatting fear. How do your trusted news sources give you facts that help you understand and grapple with problems that cause fear?

Survey News Sources

In Chapter 8, Adam Hamilton notes the findings of Dr. Shana Goldstein, a Syracuse sociologist, showing that when we are anxious we actually seek out news sources that increase our anxiety. Ask group members to call out major news outlets (for example, *USA Today, The New York Times,* local television, Facebook) where they get their news. As participants name specific news sources, write them on a large sheet of paper visible to the room. Discuss:

- Why do you go to the news sources you use? Do you find Dr. Goldstein's observation (about people seeking sources that increase their anxiety) to be true for you?
- Adam Hamilton recommends looking at a variety of news sources to help understand how others are thinking. When you intentionally seek out information and viewpoints from sources you are likely to mistrust, how do you think this would alter your experience of others?

Ask group members to choose a source on the list that they would not normally use and commit to using it before your next session. At the next group session, share experiences with this exercise.

Study the Bible Together

Chapter 7 in Hamilton's book discusses the fears that are spawned by terror attacks. After discussing how our views of terror and the danger of terrorism are often skewed, Hamilton goes on to talk about the twin challenges of preventing future attacks and exhibiting "courageous compassion" for refugees and people of other faiths.

In the section titled "An Indefinitely Suspended Welcome," Hamilton quotes Jeremiah 22:3 as a biblical warrant for helping people who come from situations of humanitarian crisis. Read or have a group member read Jeremiah 22:3 aloud:

> The LORD proclaims: Do what is just and right; rescue the oppressed from the power of the oppressor. Don't exploit or mistreat the refugee, the orphan, and the widow.

Ask the group to imagine that your group was asked to help a refugee family resettling from Syria. Divide into pairs or small groups and discuss how you would live out the biblical vision from Jeremiah in your context.

- What does doing "what is just and right" look like in this situation?
- What fears might you have to overcome in yourself or others as you welcome this refugee family?
- How might you meet God in the process?
- Why does God call us to have courageous compassion?

Test Out Thoughts About Crime

If you have collected your local crime statistics (see "Special Preparation"), have these statistics available for the next exercise. Without giving the statistics, begin by asking participants to share their general feelings about the level of violent crime in your community. Reflect on the following questions:

- Do you feel that crime is increasing, decreasing, or remaining about the same in our community?
- What helps form your impressions about the level of crime?

- If the level of crime were significantly higher or lower than you expect, what might be some reasons?

If you have the statistics, share trends over the past five to ten years. If you don't have local statistics, point to the chart included in Chapter 5, which highlights national rates of violent crime. Spend some time talking about what the statistics show.

- What do the statistics reveal about the actual levels of crime?
- What surprises you about the statistics?

In Chapter 5, Adam Hamilton talks about how distorted thinking can lead us to overestimate the threat of things such as violent crime. Among the reasons he gives for this distortion are inaccurate information, negativity, and faulty assumptions or beliefs. Hamilton talks about "cognitive restructuring" as a method of helping to identify faulty assumptions and thought patterns and replacing them with clearer thinking and better information. Discuss:

- Would knowing the actual crime statistics have affected your beliefs about crime?
- Which of the reasons Hamilton offers for distorted thinking best explain our views about crime?
- In this case, are facts really our friends? How can facts help us overcome our fears?

Get to Know Your Neighbors

In Chapter 6, Adam Hamilton talks about a street in Kansas City, Troost Avenue, that marks a dividing line between predominantly white and black communities. If you have a map of your community, place it so that it's visible to the whole group. Ask:

- Where is our community's Troost Avenue? What roads or geographic features serve as markers between different communities?
- How would you describe the perceptions of others from the perspective of those living on both sides of the marker?

- Adam Hamilton describes a lunch he had with Rev. Dr. Emmanuel Cleaver III in which they reflected on their childhood experiences growing up on different sides of Troost Avenue. What barriers are there to these kind of interactions in your community?

Invite group members to imagine taking an action to get to know neighbors across community divides. Ask volunteers to share suggestions for how this might be done. Challenge the group to act on one of these suggestions (or one of the other ideas they have heard) in the week to come.

Explore the Possibilities of a Hospitable Spectrum

In Chapter 8, Adam Hamilton asserts that most Americans fall within a broad political center and not in the extreme positions of left or right. He also talks about the vision offered by Rev. Glen Miles to describe Jesus' circle of disciples. Jesus' inner circle, says Miles, included a spectrum of views that could have been volatile.

Ask group members to name some of Jesus' closest disciples. (In Chapter 8, Hamilton talks about Matthew and Simon the Zealot.)

- What do we know about their backgrounds?
- How do you imagine they got along in the group of disciples?
- What tensions would they have had?

Now explore the current political environment in our country. The extreme positions in American politics get a lot of media attention. With that in mind, discuss:

- How accurate do you think Hamilton's observation is that most Americans don't identify with the extremes?
- Why does he say that the worry, fear, and anxiety are more prevalent as we move toward the extremes? Do you agree?

Ask a volunteer to read aloud Romans 12:18-21 (also found in the section of the chapter titled "A Help Always Near"):

If possible, to the best of your ability, live at peace with all people. Don't try to get revenge for yourselves, my dear friends, but leave room for God's wrath. It is written, *Revenge belongs to me; I will pay it back, says the Lord.* Instead, *If your enemy is hungry, feed him; if he is thirsty, give him a drink. By doing this, you will pile burning coals of fire upon his head.* Don't be defeated by evil, but defeat evil with good.

Discuss:

- What does this passage tell us about living with people with whom we disagree?
- If we took this passage seriously, what would change about our approach to those who may have different political beliefs?

Wrapping Up

Before the closing activity, tell participants that next week's session will be based on Part Three (Chapters 9–12) of the *Unafraid* book. Ask them to read as much of Part Three as they can during the coming week.

Closing Activity

Near the end of Chapter 5, Adam Hamilton describes the spiritual practice of *lectio divina,* or "divine reading," as a means of addressing the fourth point of his FEAR acronym: "Release your cares to God." Allow time (at least ten minutes) for the group to experience this practice as your closing activity.

Direct the group's attention to the appendix of Hamilton's book, where they will find thirty-one passages (one for each day of the month) that address the subject of fear. Invite participants to note the passage for today's day of the month.

Explain that you will be using a modified form of *lectio divina* that Hamilton describes. Instruct participants to settle into a comfortable position and to pray silently the prayer you will offer. Pray aloud for the group to hear: "Lord, I long to hear from you. Speak to me through these words of Scripture. I'm listening, Lord."

Ask group members to read the selected passage on their own, slowly and silently. Allow sufficient time for this reading, and then invite them to pray again with you silently as you pray aloud: "Lord, speak to me; your servant is listening."

Now instruct participants to listen as you read the passage aloud slowly, noting words or phrases that speak to them. After a period of silence, invite the group to repeat after you as you offer the two lines of the prayer aloud: "Lord, speak to me; your servant is listening."

Ask participants to read the passage a third time silently, underlining the parts that are especially meaningful. Allow time for this activity, then invite them to pray their own individual prayers silently, incorporating the words and phrases they have underlined. After a period of silence, pray the word "Amen" aloud to close the exercise.

Closing Prayer

In the closing section of Chapter 7, Hamilton quotes the second verse of the hymn "God of Grace and God of Glory." Invite group members to read that verse with you as a closing prayer for the session.

3

FAILURE, DISAPPOINTING OTHERS, INSIGNIFICANCE, AND LONELINESS

Planning the Session

Session Goals

As a result of conversations and activities connected with this session, group members should begin to

- explore courage and how its presence in social interactions helps to overcome fear;
- understand grace as a theological concept related to acceptance;

- examine the fears that social media habits can exacerbate; and
- connect "meaning-making" with the practices of faith.

Scriptural Foundation

You hem me in, behind and before,
 and lay your hand upon me. ...

Where can I go from your spirit?
 Or where can I flee from your presence?
If I ascend to heaven, you are there;
 if I make my bed in Sheol, you are there.
If I take the wings of the morning
 and settle at the farthest limits of the sea,
even there your hand shall lead me,
 and your right hand shall hold me fast.
     (Psalm 139:5, 7-10 NRSV)

Special Preparation

- Have Bibles, paper, pens, and pencils available for use.
- If you did not retain the sheet from the last session, write the points of the FEAR acronym (printed below) on a large sheet of paper and hang it in a visible location for your group. Hold on to the paper for use in future sessions.

  Face your fears with faith.
  Examine your assumptions in light of the facts.
  Attack your anxieties with action.
  Release your cares to God.

- Prepare another large sheet of paper for posting in a visible location for the group. Title it "Dealing with the Fear of Failure." Beneath the title write these three principles, which are described in Chapter 9:

  1. Most things are never as hard as you fear they will be.
  2. Successful people are willing to do the things that unsuccessful people are unwilling to do.
  3. More often than not, choosing the harder, riskier, inconvenient path is the right choice.

Getting Started

Opening Activity

In the last session, the news sources exercise included challenging group members to choose a news source they would not normally use and try using it. Invite volunteers to report back on this exercise. Discuss briefly:

- How did the news source confirm or contradict your preconceptions of it?
- In what ways, if any, did it change your understanding of an event or person in the news?
- Is this an exercise you feel you will repeat? Why or why not?

Opening Prayer

Begin by noting the observation from Chapter 12 that smartphones are having a significant impact on the mental health and feelings of loneliness in the youngest generations. Ask people to take out their cell phone, if they have one, and cradle it in their hands in front of them. (You can acknowledge, in a light-hearted way, that even today not everyone has a smartphone. If they do not have a phone, ask them to imagine that they are holding a phone they usually use.) Tell group members to reflect silently on the impact their phone has on their life. Ask the following questions for their reflection:

- How often do you pick up this phone each day? What do you use it for?
- How many calls do you receive or make? How often do you text? How often do you play a game or surf the web? How often do you check social media?
- Since you got this phone, how have your connections with other people changed? Do you feel more or less connected to others in significant ways?

Now ask the group members to imagine that the phone can connect them to God. Say: Listen in silence for what God is saying to you, then speak your fears to God in silence.

Close the time of silence by offering the following prayer aloud:

Lord, you speak throughout the cosmos and in the depths of our being. You know the desperate ways we long to be connected and the patterns of distraction that fill our days. Take the fears that we speak. Hear the deeper desires of our hearts. Be among us and between us as we search for each other and for you. Amen.

Learning Together

Video Study and Discussion

In video Session 3, Adam Hamilton discusses the fear of failure, loneliness, and rejection with his guests, Carlos, Ginger, and Marie. He also talks with Christian Cid, the CEO and president of the Serenity Counseling Center in Gallatin, Tennessee, about helping people overcome their fears.

- What did Carlos, Ginger, and Marie learn by facing their fears of failure?
- Why did Ginger feel that social media was not sufficient to help people feel connected to others?
- How did Christian Cid describe codependency? Why is it unhealthy?
- How does faith help us address our sense of meaning?

Book and Bible Study and Discussion

Reflect on Failure and Risk

In Chapter 9, Adam Hamilton explores the fear of failure and the shame and loss we associate with it. He also quotes the author J.K. Rowling, who overcame her fear of failure by recognizing that "it is impossible to live without failing at something" and then risked failure in order to achieve her goals.

Declare the space where you are meeting a "judgment-free zone," where people can be open about their failures. Invite volunteers to share brief stories of a time when their fears of failing at something were realized. (Be prepared to model what you are asking for by having a story of your own ready to share.) Thank the volunteers for their courage in sharing and then explore the stories with these questions:

- What were the consequences of your failure? Were they as extreme as you anticipated they would be?
- How did you grow from the experience? What did you learn about your own capacity to handle failure?
- What keeps us from taking the risks we need to take in order to find courage and confidence?

Point out the sheet on "Dealing with the Fear of Failure" that you prepared before the class (see "Special Preparation"). Ask the class, in light of the conversation you've been having, to comment on the three listed principles.

- Based on your own experience, how accurate are these principles?
- What other principles would you add or substitute?

Study Scripture Together

In Chapter 10, Adam Hamilton describes how, during the last presidential elections, he asked members of his congregation to memorize two Bible verses and print them on cards to carry with them.

Ask volunteers to read those two verses: Matthew 7:12 and James 1:19 from the Bible. (They are also printed in Chapter 10 in the section titled "Quick to Listen, Slow to Speak.") It may be helpful to read the verses from the book or from this leader guide, since you will want a common translation for the next exercise.

"You should treat people in the same way that you want people to treat you."

(Matthew 7:12a)

Be quick to listen, slow to speak, and slow to grow angry.

(James 1:19b)

Now ask all the group members to find a partner and work on memorizing the verses using the following method:

- Read one verse aloud together.
- Alternating between you and your partner, say the verse aloud, as best you can, without reading it. (Your partner can prompt if needed.)
- Keep alternating in this manner until both of you can say the verse comfortably without prompting.
- Repeat the process with the second verse.

Return to the large group and go around the circle, encouraging each participant to say the verses aloud from memory. Ask the group to reflect on the verses using the following questions:

- Where in our nation or community do we see persons living out the ethic expressed in these verses?
- In what situations is it most difficult to live this out?
- Where do you see Jesus and other Biblical characters exhibiting this behavior?

As a group, without reading the verses, recite them again before moving on to the next exercise.

Discuss Social Media Challenges

In Chapter 10, Adam Hamilton discusses the ways that online interactions, especially through social media, can open us up to criticism and rejection. Invite group members to call out the social media platforms in which they participate. Ask volunteers to share briefly a time when they have felt seen, affirmed, or cared for by social media interactions.

- What happened? What was its impact on you?

Now ask volunteers once again to share briefly a time when they or others they know have been injured by something posted on social media.

- What happened? What impact did it have?
- How does it feel to post something and get no reaction?

Ask the group:

- How should we react to painful comments and rejection in our online lives?
- What strategies does Hamilton suggest for building our resilience and reducing our need to please others?

Do a Theological Word Study on Grace

Some of our unhealthy patterns of trying to please others, according to Adam Hamilton, result from our need for acceptance, including acceptance from God. Hamilton points to grace as the theological concept that can lead us to a healthier relationship with God and others.

Ask group members to reflect on where they hear the term *grace* in everyday life. (Responses might include the "grace" said before a meal, a "grace period" for turning in late assignments, someone with a "gracious spirit," or a dancer who moves with "grace.")

Share Hamilton's definition of grace (found in the section of Chapter 10 titled "How Grace Saves Us"):

> Grace is undeserved kindness, blessing, mercy, and love.
> Grace is grace precisely because we can't earn it.

Form small groups of about three people and ask each group to explore one of the following Bible passages: Genesis 1:27-31, Psalm 23, Luke 23:39-43, and Ephesians 2:4-9. Ask them to use this question as they read the assigned passage:

- What does this passage tell us about the nature of God's grace?

After some minutes of discussion, come back as a large group and share insights from the small group conversation.

Next have a volunteer read the paragraphs from Paul Tillich's sermon "You are Accepted," which are found in the same section of Chapter 10. Ask:

- What is most hopeful about Tillich's words?

- How does God's acceptance of us through grace free us from the fear of disappointing others?
- What practices help you remember God's acceptance of you?

Complete the Sentence to Explore Meaning

When businesses and organizations do strategic planning, they often revisit their purpose statement and look at their practices. Part of this exercise frequently includes challenging themselves to complete the following sentence: "We are doing this because ..." If the sentence they create is congruent with their mission, they feel confident in continuing it. If not, it is a signal to change what they are doing. Lovett Weems of the Lewis Center for Church Leadership at Wesley Theological Seminary has a similar framing for churches.*

Individuals can do a similar exercise. Invite group members to use the paper and writing instruments available. Ask them to think of a daily practice or activity they engage in and to complete the following sentence: "I am doing this practice because ..."

After participants have done the exercise, help them reflect on what they have learned. Ask:

- Are you satisfied with the statement you wrote?
- Does it lead you to other questions about the role of this practice in your life?
- How does this practice draw me closer or away from God's love and intentions for me?
- What change could you make that would help you toward a more meaningful practice?

Examine the Impact of Loneliness

In Chapter 12, Adam Hamilton discusses the "epidemic of loneliness" that many Americans are experiencing. The beginning of the chapter discusses the "attachment theory" of John Bowles and the three types of attachment he identified: secure, anxious, and avoidant.

---

*Read a review of Lovett Weems's book *Bearing Fruit: Ministry with Real Results* at https://www.umcdiscipleship.org/resources/review-of-bearing-fruit-ministry-with-real-results-by-lovett-h.-weems-jr.-a

Ask participants to review or read aloud the section of Chapter 12 titled "God's First 'Not Good.'" Ask group members to reflect on Hamilton's observation that we all need human connection:

- How is human connection under stress in contemporary America?
- Where do you see loneliness in your community? in your life?
- With which of the three types of attachment do you most closely identify? (Be aware that some people may not be comfortable answering this last question. Do not press each person to answer.)

Direct the group's attention to the FEAR acronym that you posted before the session in the meeting space. Have the group read it aloud with you. Regarding the particular fear of being alone and unnoticed, imagine how you would use the steps of the acronym to talk with yourself about this fear:

- What faith resources do I have to address this fear?
- How realistic are the fears?
- What actions might I take to attack my anxieties?
- What practices would help me release my cares to God?

Wrapping Up

Before the closing activity, tell participants that next week's session will be based on Part Four (Chapters 13–16) of the *Unafraid* book. Ask them to read as much of Part Four as they can during the coming week.

Closing Activity

In Chapter 12, under the heading "Learning to Reengage," Adam Hamilton offers some practical suggestions for reaching out to others and overcoming our fears of not being able to connect. Review some of the suggestions with the class (reengage with others despite our initial discomfort, invest in relationships, visit those who are lonely, get involved in our church or faith community).

Ask participants to spend a few minutes silently reflecting on these suggestions and considering one action they might take this week to move toward one of them. Invite the group members to commit to that action by writing it down on a piece of paper that they will take with them.

Closing Prayer

As a group, recite again the verses you memorized during the session:

> "You should treat people in the same way that you want people to treat you."
>
> (Matthew 7:12a)

> Be quick to listen, slow to speak, and slow to grow angry.
>
> (James 1:19b)

Now read aloud the verses from Psalm 139 that are printed at the end of Chapter 12 as a closing prayer. Remind group members that the grace revealed in Jesus Christ gives us confidence that God is present with us always.

> You hem me in, behind and before,
>   and lay your hand upon me. ...
>
> Where can I go from your spirit?
>   Or where can I flee from your presence?
> If I ascend to heaven, you are there;
>   if I make my bed in Sheol, you are there.
> If I take the wings of the morning
>   and settle at the farthest limits of the sea,
> even there your hand shall lead me,
>   and your right hand shall hold me fast.
>
> (Psalm 139:5, 7-10 NRSV)

4

APOCALYPSE, CHANGE, MISSING OUT, AND FINANCES

Planning the Session

Session Goals

As a result of conversations and activities connected with this session, group members should begin to

- understand apocalyptic expectations in light of biblical visions about God's ultimate victory;
- investigate how grief may be informing our fear of change;
- appreciate how the practice of cultivating gratitude can address our feelings of fear and discontent; and
- explore how sound financial principles can alleviate financial anxiety.

Scriptural Foundation

"Therefore I tell you, do not worry about your life, what you will eat, or about your body, what you will wear. For life is more than food, and the body more than clothing. ... Consider the lilies, how they grow: they neither toil nor spin; yet I tell you, even Solomon in all his glory was not clothed like one of these. But if God so clothes the grass of the field, which is alive today and tomorrow is thrown into the oven, how much more will he clothe you—you of little faith! And do not keep striving for what you are to eat and what you are to drink, and do not keep worrying. For it is the nations of the world that strive after all these things, and your Father knows that you need them. Instead, strive for his kingdom, and these things will be given to you as well."

(Luke 12:22-23, 27-31 NRSV)

Special Preparation

- If you did not retain the sheet from the last session, write the points of the FEAR acronym (printed below) on a large sheet of paper and hang it in a visible location for your group. Hold on to the paper for use in future sessions.

  Face your fears with faith.
  Examine your assumptions in light of the facts.
  Attack your anxieties with action.
  Release your cares to God.

- Post a large sheet of blank paper next to the FEAR acronym. Have markers available.
- Have Bibles, paper, pens, and pencils available for use.

Getting Started

Opening Activity

Each fall, as college freshmen head to school, surveys pop up describing the incoming class. Usually the surveys emphasize how many old technologies are unfamiliar to them (for instance, many may have never used a VCR) or what events older people may still think of as current that the students regard as history (such as the Iraq War, which began when they were toddlers).

Ask the group to imagine trying to describe the world you grew up in to someone who is twenty years old. What things would they not have known about? What important buildings are no longer standing or have been repurposed? What influential people died before they were born? How much change has taken place since the years when you grew up?

Explain that in this session we will be exploring trends and changes that cause many people to experience anxiety and worry. The purpose of this session is to help us embrace the confidence and trust embodied in Jesus' words in Luke 12:22-23, 27-31 (printed in the "Scriptural Foundation"). Ask a volunteer to read those verses aloud.

Opening Prayer

Pray together, using the following prayer or one of your own choosing:

God of every age, you know that the more things change, the more things stay the same. Help us to face our fears with faith and to see in our time together the ways you are calling us to trust in you. We do not want to hold these worries; we want to be held in your hand. Amen.

Learning Together

Video Study and Discussion

In video Session 4, Adam Hamilton talks about apocalyptic thinking with his guests, Carlos, Ginger, and Marie. He also interviews Jerre Stead about the role that uncertainty plays in business planning. Stead is Chairman and CEO of IHS Market Ltd. and was formerly Chairman and CEO of Ingram Micro Inc. Ask:

- How does our relationship with technology affect our thinking about the future?

- How did Ginger experience a change in her thinking about financial insecurity?
- Why did Jerre Stead feel that communication was critical in helping his workers face uncertainty?
- Why does Jerre Stead feel that "facts are our friends"? How do facts influence our actions?

Book and Bible Study and Discussion

Explore Our Fascination with the End of the World

Ask group members to throw out titles of popular entertainment (books, TV, movies) that feature an end-of-the-world scenario. Some examples might be *Independence Day*, *The Walking Dead*, and *The Road*. Ask group members who enjoy this kind of entertainment to share why they find it appealing.

In Chapter 13, Adam Hamilton suggests that apocalyptic and dystopian visions are popular because they draw on our fears about the future. This can be seen in the causes of the catastrophes in our entertainment. Invite participants to share some of the causes of disaster in apocalyptic movies. If necessary you can prompt with these examples—climate change, nuclear war, global pandemic, or alien invasion. Ask:

- How do you feel when you see depictions of your fears about the future coming to reality?
- Is there something useful about facing those fears through popular culture?

Now ask the group to review or read the section of Chapter 13 titled "Ending with Paradise Restored."

- What are the elements of the biblical vision of the new heaven and the new earth?
- How might this vision of God's future change the stories we tell about the present?

46

In this section, Hamilton notes two negative responses we might make to the problems of the day: (1) not caring about the problems because God will eventually bring about a new heaven and a new earth, and (2) being paralyzed by the problems because we forget that God will ultimately prevail. Ask:

- Which of these errors do you feel is more prominent among Christians?
- To which of these responses are you more prone?
- If we took God's promise of ultimate restoration seriously, how would it affect our behavior in the present?

Use the Acronym to Analyze a Fear

Read the section of Chapter 13 titled "Starting with a Bias of Hope." Point out to the group Hamilton's FEAR acronym that you posted in a visible place before the session began.

Invite the group to use the principles named in the acronym to analyze a fear we might have about the future. For instance, you might use the fear of nuclear war, which is discussed in Chapter 13. Ask group members to close their eyes for a few moments and reflect on how they feel when they think about this problem.

On the large blank sheet of paper you've posted, write group responses to the following questions under the appropriate letter:

F*ace your fears with faith.*
- o   How does our faith help us confront this fear?
- o   What institutions, systems, and safeguards are in place to prevent the thing we fear?

E*xamine your assumptions in light of the facts.*
- o   What information could we seek that might help us challenge or confirm our assumptions about this problem?

A*ttack your anxieties with action.*
- o   What actions could we take that might help deal with this problem?

Release your cares to God.

   o   What spiritual practices would help us release this fear to God?

After completing the exercise, invite participants to close their eyes again and reflect on how they feel about this problem. After a few moments, invite sharing from the group about their reflections.

Study Scripture Together

Invite a volunteer to do some acting. Tell the volunteer that she or he will be improvising lines while playing the man waiting by the Pool of Bethsaida who was healed by Jesus. (We'll read the story in a moment.) If the volunteer is able and willing, have that person stretch out on the floor in the center of the group for this exercise. (The exercise works without this posture as well.)

Now have a volunteer read John 5:2-9 from the Bible. Invite the group to imagine that they are reporters sent to interview the man who was healed. Have them ask questions about why the man is there and what it has felt like for him to be there. Ask the volunteer to respond in character. Encourage the group to have fun and not feel there are "right" ways to do this.

Allow several minutes for the exercise. Thank the volunteer, and have the person move out of character and back into the circle. Then reflect as a group on the exercise:

- What were some of the reasons given for the man's illness?
- What others might you imagine?
- Why might Jesus have asked him, "Do you want to get well?"

In Chapter 14, Adam Hamilton notes that we can sometimes be uncomfortable with difficult situations because we are afraid of what a change might mean for us. Invite volunteers to share briefly a time when they resisted addressing a situation because they were afraid. What happened when you did confront it? Ask the whole group:

- How did Jesus address the man's condition?
- If Jesus were talking to you about getting beyond a fear that is distressing you, what do you think he would say to you?

Read the final section of Chapter 14, titled "New Joys on the Other Side." Preface your reading by reminding the group that Hamilton is talking about the grief he felt when his daughters left for college. Ask:

- How does faith give us the capacity to change?

Examine Ways to Put Social Media in Proper Perspective

In the previous session we explored how social media can amplify feelings of rejection and loneliness. In Chapter 15, Adam Hamilton returns to social media to look at how it can increase our fear of missing out (FOMO).

Read aloud the section of Chapter 15 titled "The Perfect Anxiety-Producing Machine." Ask the group:

- Why does Hamilton feel that social media is an "anxiety-producing machine"?
- What two ways does he offer for addressing FOMO with regard to social media?

Distribute paper and writing instruments to participants. Ask them to think back to yesterday and write down a list of their activities. (Assure them they will not be asked to share what they write.) Who were you with? Where did you go? Allow several minutes for this activity.

Now ask the group to go back through their list and choose which of their listed activities they might have considered sharing with others through social media. Did you see a beautiful sunset? Were you with a friend you hadn't seen in a while? Would you take a picture of the meal you ordered at a restaurant? How many of your activities would have made "good" posts on social media? After eliminating those activities, what's left? Again, allow some time for this activity.

Finally, ask group members to choose one of the remaining activities (those you felt would not have made "good" posts) and imagine posting that activity on a social media site. If you were being honest in the post, what would you say about this activity and how you were feeling? Invite volunteers to share one of these imagined posts. Ask:

- What, in anything, did you learn from this exercise about the "anxiety-producing machine"?
- What do you think makes a "good" post, and what does not? Why?
- What new perspectives on social media, if any, did you gain from the exercise?

Consider Financial Principles

In Chapter 16, Adam Hamilton writes about ways to approach financial anxieties. In the closing section, titled "The Right Kind of Financial Fear," he introduces five financial principles to help move us toward a simpler, sustainable lifestyle. Read this section aloud (or have volunteers read it), up through and including the list of principles.

Invite group members to reflect on which of these five principles they are currently using in their own lives. Move through the list and ask if there is anyone who would like to share a testimony about how a particular principle has helped ease financial anxieties or how the group members are struggling in this area. Affirm for the group that very few people in our society are consistently using these principles, and so the struggles are widespread. If anyone does share that they are having significant difficulties, thank them for their courage and, perhaps afterward, offer ideas for resources, including the pastors of your church.

Ask participants to choose one of the principles they would most like to work toward. Ask: What is one action you could take this week to help move toward living this out? Invite volunteers to share their commitments.

Wrapping Up

Before the closing activity, tell participants that next week's session will be based on Part Five (Chapters 17–20) of the *Unafraid* book. Ask them to read as much of Part Five as they can during the coming week.

Closing Activity

In Chapter 15, Adam Hamilton talks about the practice of cultivating gratitude as a way of retraining our minds to "want what we already have." Invite group members into a closing time of offering thanks for the things they have. Read aloud 1 Thessalonians 5:16 ("Rejoice always.") and ask them to consider how they can "give thanks in every situation."

Now read aloud the following litany and ask group members to follow each sentence with the phrase, "*We give you thanks, O Lord!*"

When the morning is bright with possibility . . .
When the day is dark and the skies are heavy . . .
When children remind us of your promises for the future . . .
When the car makes strange noises on the way to work . . .
When we receive an unexpected gift . . .
When the bill is more than we expected and the bank account is low . . .
When we lose unwanted pounds on the scale . . .
When weariness and illness drag us down . . .
When a moment with a friend makes us want to share the joy . . .
When a memory of past hurts brings us feelings of shame . . .
In joy, in sorrow, in good times and bad, in life, in death . . .

Closing Prayer

Pray the following prayer or one of your own:

God of lilies and sparrows and the grass of the field, we hear your call to spend no worry on the things we call necessity. We want to trust in you. We release our cares to you. We walk into the future knowing we are in your hands. And in all things we give you thanks. Amen.

5

AGING, ILLNESS, DYING, AND FEAR OF THE LORD

Planning the Session

Session Goals

As a result of conversations and activities connected with this session, group members should begin to

- develop a sense of confidence that God gives new dreams and even joy in old age;
- appreciate mindfulness as a practice that helps address anxiety;
- explore Christian themes and beliefs about death and heaven; and
- understand the biblical concept of fear of the Lord as the grounds for trust in God.

Scriptural Foundation

Don't be anxious about anything; rather, bring up all of your requests to God in your prayers and petitions, along with giving thanks. Then the peace of God that exceeds all understanding will keep your hearts and minds safe in Christ Jesus.

(Philippians 4:6-7)

Special Preparation

- Arrange seating in a circle.
- If you did not retain the sheet from the last session, write the points of the FEAR acronym (printed below) on a large sheet of paper and hang it in a visible location for your group.

  *F*ace *your fears with faith.*
  *E*xamine *your assumptions in light of the facts.*
  *A*ttack *your anxieties with action.*
  *R*elease *your cares to God.*

- Have Bibles available for the group to use.
- Post two large sheets of blank paper in a visible place in your meeting area. Have markers available for use.
- Have available copies of published liturgies for a funeral service or memorial service.

Getting Started

Opening Activity

In Chapter 18, Adam Hamilton introduces the concept of *mindfulness* as a practice to address worry. After group members have arrived, introduce the opening activity by having a volunteer read the first paragraph of the section titled "What We Gain from Mindfulness."

Acknowledge that you and the participants have entered the room with all sorts of things on your minds that keep you from being present in the moment. Tell them that the "four-sided" or "square breathing" method of mindfulness recommended by James Cochran (quoted following the passage you just read) is designed to help them become mindful of the present moment by paying attention to breathing.

Invite group members to get into a comfortable position with an open body posture (legs uncrossed, arms relaxed). Have them close their eyes and follow the instructions you will give aloud. Give these instructions at a pace that allows them to be followed easily. (Don't count to four too slowly!) Read these instructions as written:

Breathe in slowly as I count: 1 ... 2 ... 3 ... 4 ...
Hold your breath as I count: 1 ... 2 ... 3 ... 4 ...
Exhale slowly as I count: 1 ... 2 ... 3 ... 4 ...
Hold with your lungs empty: 1 ... 2 ... 3 ... 4 ...
Repeat the practice several times.

Then invite class members to breathe normally, keeping their eyes closed for the prayer to follow.

Opening Prayer

Pray together, using the following prayer or one of your own:

God who breathed life into the first human in Eden, you are as near to us as our own breath. Your Spirit moves within us and around us. We are grateful for this moment and this day. Take our fears and worries about tomorrow and our regrets and hurts we carry from yesterday. We release ourselves and our time to you. Amen.

Learning Together

Video Study and Discussion

In video Session 5, Adam Hamilton explores fears of death and illness with his guests, Carlos, Ginger, and Marie. He also welcomes his spouse, LaVon Hamilton, a sign language interpreter, to discuss her own struggles with anxiety.

- How has Ginger faced the challenges of her multiple sclerosis? What role has her faith played?
- How did the group members' experience with people facing death affect their own experience with fears of death?

- What steps did LaVon Hamilton take to determine that the problem she was dealing with was anxiety?
- How did LaVon's faith that her life was in the hands of her Savior help her overcome anxiety?

Book and Bible Study and Discussion

Use the Story of Siddhartha to Explore Angst

In the interlude that begins Part Five, Adam Hamilton relates the story of Siddhartha, who as a young man was deeply troubled when confronted with the realities of old age, illness, and death. Hamilton uses the term *angst* to describe the feelings we have when we consider these existential concerns.

Ask the group to recall one of the first occasions when they were confronted with the realities that Siddhartha discovered about life and death.

- What was the occasion (such as the death of a pet or grandparent, a parent's injury or illness)? How did it affect you?
- Who helped you deal with what you were feeling?

Tell the group that this session is designed to help us look at distinctively Christian ways to approach these realities and the fears we have about them.

Study a Bible Story with Elderly Characters

In Chapter 17, Adam Hamilton lifts up biblical stories of God working through older adults. Invite group members to call out characters in the Bible who did remarkable things at advanced ages. (Hamilton lists some in the section titled "Clara and Great-Aunt Celia on a Mission.")

Now ask group members to read along or listen to Luke 2:25-38 as a volunteer reads it aloud. Afterward, consider Simeon and Anna.

- What does the Bible tell us about whom they were?
- What role do they play in the story of Jesus?

- How were they using their time in old age?
- How are they models for thinking about God's intentions for us in old age?

Consider the Possibilities of Old Age

Point out the large sheet with the FEAR acronym that you posted in a visible place prior to the session. Invite the group to consider how the principles of the acronym might be used in considering our worries about aging.

Give each person a letter of the acronym (F, E, A, or R) and advise them that we will go around the circle and invite each person to offer a reflection based on the principle associated with that part of the acronym. For instance, if my letter is F the principle associated with it is "Face your fears with faith," and I might respond with the Bible verse Adam Hamilton notes in Chapter 17: "Your old men [and women] will dream dreams" (from Joel 2:28 and repeated in Acts 2:17).

Offer the following guiding questions to help people in forming their responses:

F*ace your fears with faith.*
o How does my faith or the Bible help me face the fear of aging?

E*xamine your assumptions in light of the facts.*
o What things did I believe about aging as a younger person that have turned out not to be true?

A*ttack your anxieties with action.*
o What is something I can do to make aging less scary?

R*elease your cares to God.*
o What practices or prayers will help me release my cares to God?

Learn from Studies of Seniors

In the section titled "When Older = Happier" in Chapter 17, Adam Hamilton notes that, according to surveys, people in their seventies or older are often among the happiest. Ask a volunteer to read the bulleted list of reasons in this section aloud. Invite participants to respond to the list with their own observations.

- Which of the reasons seems surprising?
- When have you seen some of these reasons confirmed?
- What other reasons would you add to the list?

Analyze a Pharmaceutical Advertisement

In Chapter 18, Adam Hamilton says that pharmaceutical companies spend billions of dollars every year to market to consumers. Invite a volunteer to describe a drug advertisement that they have seen on television or the Internet recently. Now, have the group call out features of a typical advertisement of this type. Discuss:

- What fears do these ads play on? What positive effects might they have?
- What promises are made about the impact of the drug on our lives?
- What potential side effects are mentioned?
- What visuals accompany the words of the ad?

Now, brainstorm your own advertisement. Imagine that you are group of marketers who have been asked to come up with an ad for prayer as a response to the problem of worry about illness. Have a volunteer write responses to the following questions on a large blank sheet of paper that is visible in your meeting area.

- What promises does God make about prayer? (You may want to include a few Bible verses.)
- What visuals will accompany your ad?
- What side effects are possible?

If your group is particularly creative, create or act out the advertisement you have constructed.

Discuss LaVon's Story

In Chapter 18, LaVon Hamilton discusses her own experience with an anxiety disorder in the section titled "Chasing Anxiety Disorder Out into the Light." Have the group read aloud the paragraphs LaVon wrote, with a different reader taking each paragraph. Share initial reactions to the story. Discuss:

- If you had the symptoms LaVon describes, would you consider that anxiety might be involved?
- How familiar are you with anxiety disorders?
- What do you appreciate about the way LaVon relates her experience?

In this section, LaVon shares some specific techniques she used and continues to use to manage her anxiety. Ask the group to identify those techniques in the paragraphs you have read. (Some of them are: meeting with a trained counselor, medication, helping others, finding activities that gave her peace, and staying close to her faith.) Which of these techniques could be helpful in dealing with milder forms of anxiety? Which have you found helpful in your own life?

Explore Principles for Dealing with Serious Illness

In the sections of Chapter 18 titled "Facing Real Maladies with Courage and Hope" and "Allen's Story," Adam Hamilton shares the stories of three people who faced serious illness. In this part of the chapter, he lifts up some approaches that these people found helpful:

- Trust that my life belongs to God.
- Serve others.
- Live one day at a time.
- Give thanks for each day.
- Remember the death and resurrection of Jesus.

Read each of these aloud, and ask a volunteer to write them on a large sheet of blank paper that you posted earlier in your meeting space. Ask group members to respond to the following questions:

- As you imagine the difficulties of facing serious illness, which of these feels like the most difficult to do? Which seem surprising?
- Which, if any, of these principles, are you following now?

Explore Christian Beliefs about Death and Heaven

In Chapter 19, Adam Hamilton addresses Christian beliefs about death and heaven. Review the section titled "The Christian View of Death and What Comes After." Ask:

- In what ways is this vision of death different from the visions we see in popular culture?

If you have made copies of a published liturgy for a funeral service or memorial service, hand them out (see "Special Preparation"). Most liturgies of this type include elements that reflect Christian beliefs about death and the afterlife. Discuss the elements in this particular liturgy:

- What beliefs about death and the afterlife are expressed or implied?
- What Scriptures are used? What do these express, and in what ways do they offer comfort?
- What other elements are notable, and what do we learn from them?
- If you were in the family of the deceased, how would you respond to this liturgy?

Examine God's Purposes

In the first paragraph of the Chapter 20 section titled "Finding God in the Storms," Adam Hamilton writes, "I don't believe, despite what property insurance policies might say, that natural disasters are 'acts of God.'" He goes on to say that some events appear to go against God's will, but God can bend those events to serve God's purposes. For example, he describes good things that have emerged following the devastation of hurricanes. Discuss:

- When have you seen good emerge from events that were destructive?
- What comfort have you found in trusting that God works for good even in terrible situations?
- How does this trust reflect awe and reverence for God?

Wrapping Up

Closing Activity

Since this is your final session, invite group members to consider how they have learned to be less afraid through the course of this study. Share Adam Hamilton's summary about fear from Chapter 20, in which he states that living unafraid doesn't mean living without fear; rather, it means living without being controlled by fear.

Tell the group that you will be going around the circle and inviting each person to share something they will take away from the study that has been helpful to them in addressing fear, worry, or anxiety. If someone does not wish to share, invite him or her to pass to the next person in the circle. Begin the sharing yourself.

Closing Prayer

Pray the following prayer or one of your own:

Lord of life and conqueror of death, you have shown us how to confront the fears we face each day. From the terrors of the night, to the future we cannot see, you have promised to be with us. We thank you for the community we have shared together and the strength we have drawn from each other. We go forth to live unafraid with love for you and for our neighbors. In the strong name of Jesus. Amen.

CPSIA information can be obtained
at www.ICGtesting.com
Printed in the USA
LVHW031000140420
653397LV00024B/2978